daybook, *n.* a book in which the events of the day are recorded; *specif.* a journal or diary

DAYBOOK
of Critical Reading and Writing

AUTHOR

VICKI SPANDEL

CONSULTING AUTHORS

RUTH NATHAN

LAURA ROBB

Great Source Education Group
a Houghton Mifflin Company
Wilmington, Massachusetts

AUTHOR

VICKI SPANDEL, director of Write Traits, provides training to writing teachers both nationally and internationally. A former teacher and journalist, Vicki is author of more than twenty books, including the new third edition of *Creating Writers.*

CONSULTING AUTHORS

RUTH NATHAN, one of the authors of *Writers Express* and *Write Away,* is the author of many professional books and articles on literacy. She currently teaches in third grade as well as consults with numerous schools and organizations on reading.

LAURA ROBB, author of *Reading Strategies That Work* and *Teaching Reading in Middle School,* has taught language arts at Powhatan School in Boyce, Virginia, for more than thirty years. She also mentors and coaches teachers in Virginia public schools and speaks at conferences throughout the country.

Printed in the United States of America

International Standard Book Number: 0-669-48036-3

2 3 4 5 6 7 8 9 10 - BA - 06 05 04 03 02 01

3

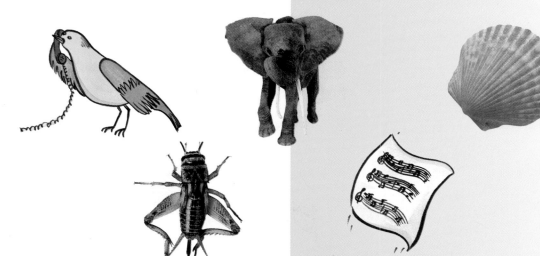

TABLE OF CONTENTS

7

Active Reading

Do you have friends who are always on the move? Are they always doing something? Active readers are always doing something too. They predict, question, and visualize. Active readers mark up the text by circling, underlining, and taking notes.

This book will help you become a more active reader. You'll learn and practice different strategies for getting involved with your reading. And, when you get involved with what you read, you'll find you understand and remember more of what you read.

Mark Up the Text

Active readers mark up the text when they come across important ideas or other things they want to remember. Then, if they need to look back at what they read, their eyes will automatically go to the marked up areas. To mark up, you might underline, circle, or star. (Remember: only mark up your own books, not books belonging to the school or library.) Here's how one reader marked up the first few paragraphs of a story.

Response Notes

Example:

What a name!

! ! !

Good idea ✱

from ***A Mouse Called Wolf***
by Dick King-Smith

Wolfgang Amadeus Mouse was the youngest of thirteen children. He was also the smallest. His mother had given the other twelve mouse pups quite ordinary names, like Bill or Jane.

But when she looked at her last-born and saw that he was only half as big as his brothers and sisters, she said to herself, ✱"He should have an important sounding name to make up for his lack of size. On second thought, he should have two important-sounding names. But what should they be?"

10

Predict

Active readers predict what's going to happen before they read and while they read. It helps them get involved in the story. Here are one reader's predictions for the next part of *A Mouse Called Wolf*. To make predictions, use what you already know and clues from the story to figure out what will happen next.

from *A Mouse Called Wolf*
by Dick King-Smith

Now, it so happened that this particular mother mouse lived in a house belonging to a lady who played the piano. It was a grand piano that stood close to a living room wall, so that its left front leg almost touched the molding. In the molding, hidden from the human eye by the piano leg, was a hole. In this hole lived the mother mouse (whose name was Mary).

One night, when the lady of the house had played a final tune on the piano and gone to bed, Mary came out of the hole in the molding. She ran up the left front leg and onto the keyboard, which as usual had been left open, and bounced along over the keys. But even though she was heavy with young, she was still much too light to make any noise.

Response Notes

Example:

Will his name have something to do with the piano?

11

Active readers also ask questions when they're reading. Do you sometimes ask questions about things you don't understand, like unfamiliar words or ideas? Do you ever question why a character does something or how a story turns out? Here's how one reader asked questions while reading the next part of *A Mouse Called Wolf*.

Response Notes

Example:

Who is this?

Can mice really do this?

from *A Mouse Called Wolf*
by Dick King-Smith

Then she saw that a single sheet of music had been left lying on the piano stool.

"Just what I need to start making my nest with," said Mary Mouse, and by pushing at the sheet (a piece of piano music by Mozart) with her little forepaws, she managed to send it sailing down to the floor. Because it was too big to drag through the mousehole, she cut it up into smaller pieces with her sharp teeth and pulled the pieces inside.

Over the next day Mary chewed these small pieces of paper into shreds, and with them built herself a most comfortable nest. In this, in due course, she gave birth to her thirteen pups.

12

Visualize

A ctive readers visualize, or create pictures in their heads as they read. Visualizing helps readers "see" a selection. When you visualize, you might want to draw a simple sketch or drawing.

Here's what one reader "saw" while reading the end of *A Mouse Called Wolf.*

(FYI: Wolfgang Amadeus Mozart was a famous composer.)

from *A Mouse Called Wolf*
by Dick King-Smith

Only when they were several days old, and she had made the decision that the thirteenth and littlest must have not one but two names, and important-sounding names at that, did something catch her eye.

It was a scrap of the sheet music that had somehow escaped being chewed up, and it had some writing on it.

Mary got out of her nest to inspect it. It said:

WOLFGANG AMADEUS MO

Mary gave a squeak of delight.

"Perfect!" she cried to all the blind and naked pups. Then she softly whispered in the littlest one's ear, "This name was specially designed for you, dear. I feel it in my bones. Why, to be sure, the last three letters of the third word are missing, but there's no doubt what they were. The smallest you may be, but these names will make you the greatest, Wolfgang Amadeus Mouse!"

Response Notes

Example:

13

Apply the Strategies

As you read this Daybook, try to mark up the text, predict, question, and visualize. Write in the Response Notes space beside each selection. Look back at the examples if you need help. Practice as you read the poem below. Try to use at least two of the strategies as you read "A Fire-Breathing Dragon."

Response Notes

14

A Fire-Breathing Dragon
by Douglas Florian

A fire-breathing dragon
Would make a precious pet —
It's great for grilling hot dogs
And drying clothes all wet.

It gladly guards the house and yard
From burglars in the street.
On winter nights how it delights
To warm your frozen feet.

It eats unwanted guests for lunch
And munches noisy neighbors.
Insistent salesmen at the door,
A hungry dragon savors.

A dragon is a noble beast,
A perfect primal pet.
The only trick
Is when it's sick,
Don't let it eat the vet.

You will enjoy and understand more of what you read by reading actively.

Reading Well

Good readers are thinking readers. They watch for important ideas and interesting facts. They ask questions and talk about what they've learned. Plus they have fun while they are reading. They say to themselves, "Hey! This is a funny character!" or

"Wow! This is unbelievable."

In this unit, you'll highlight, underline, and circle important ideas as you read. You'll also make guesses, ask questions, and hunt for clues.

What Will Happen Next?

Good readers make **predictions** as they read. This means they make guesses about how things will turn out. You might say things like, "I think this story will have a happy ending" or "I think this character is going to get into a lot of trouble."

Read this story about a rabbit named Solomon. As you read, ask yourself, "What will happen to Solomon?" Write your predictions in the Response Notes.

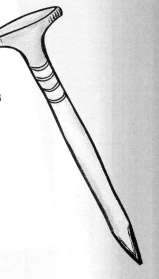

Response Notes

Example:

> I predict
> Solomon is a
> magic rabbit.

16

from *Solomon the Rusty Nail*
by William Steig

Solomon was an ordinary rabbit, except for one thing: anytime he wanted to, he could turn into a rusty nail. How did he discover he had this gift?

He was sitting on the bench by his house one day, just gazing at the world, when he happened to scratch his nose and wiggle his toes at exactly the same time. And zingo! just like that, he became something hard and tiny.

He could still hear though he had no ears, and see though he had no eyes, but he couldn't figure out what he had turned into until his mother came out to sweep up. "What is this rusty nail doing on the bench?" she said, and chucked him in the trash can.

from *Solomon the Rusty Nail*
by William Steig

He couldn't cry out "Mom, it's me!" He had no way of making a sound. Naturally, he began to worry. What would become of him? Would he wind up at the town dump with the rest of the garbage, and stay there forever? Or what?

"I don't belong in here with this junk," he said to himself. "I'm no nail, I'm a rabbit!"

17

STOP AND PREDICT

➥ **What do you think will happen to Solomon now? Use your notes to help you make your prediction.**

What I Predict Will Happen	Evidence (Clues from the Story)

Response Notes

from *Solomon the Rusty Nail*
by William Steig

The moment he thought those words, he was a rabbit again. In a daze, he climbed out of the trash can, went behind the toolshed, and sat down on the solid ground. Did what just happened really happen? It did. Dare he try to make it happen again?

He dared—over and over, until he was sure he could always do it. When he scratched his nose and wiggled his toes, he became a rusty nail. And when he thought "I'm no nail, I'm a rabbit," he was a rabbit.

STOP AND PREDICT

➥ Do you predict Solomon will show his trick to others, or will he keep it a secret? Explain.

What I Predict Will Happen	Evidence (Clues from the Story)

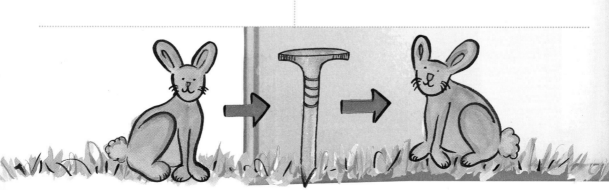

➤ Pretend you are the author of the story about Solomon the rusty nail. Use this story board to plan how the story should end. Draw pictures to **show** what happens.

1.

2.

3.

4.

19

Now, **tell** what happens. Write an ending for *Solomon the Rusty Nail*. Be sure to look at your story board as you write.

20

As you read,
ask yourself:
What do I think
will happen
next?

What's the Big Idea?

When you want to learn something new or find information, nonfiction books are a good place to look. Did you know that every nonfiction book or article has a **main idea?** The main idea is the most important idea. It is what the book or article is all about.

As you read this article about scientists, underline every important idea. Write any questions you have in the Response Notes.

Response Notes

from *How to Think Like a Scientist*
by Stephen Kramer

Scientists are people who are curious. They want to know about the things around them. They are always asking questions and trying to answer them.

Some scientists study birds. They might ask the question, "Why do meadowlarks sing?" Other scientists study objects in the universe. They might ask, "What happens to stars as they grow older?" Other scientists might ask: "What are atoms made of?" "How does gravity work?" "What lives at the bottom of the ocean?" "Why does the wind blow?" "How does the body heal itself?" Still other scientists might be interested in learning about old folktales and checking to see if any of them are true. Such a scientist might be interested in the question, "Can throwing a dead snake over a tree branch bring rain?"

Response Notes

from **How to Think Like a Scientist**
by Stephen Kramer

Scientists believe that the things around us behave in certain ways. They believe that things that happen can be described by certain rules. Scientists try to find patterns in things. They look for explanations for the patterns in the things around us.

Scientists learn about things by observing and measuring them. Science can deal only with things that can be observed. To a scientist, being able to observe something means that we can learn about it by using our senses. It can be seen, heard, smelled, touched, or tasted.

Scientists often use instruments to help them make observations. Machines and special instruments can tell us much about things we can't know by using our senses alone. But if there is no way to observe and measure something, it can't be studied scientifically.

What is one thing you learned from reading *How to Think Like a Scientist?*

➤ There are lots of ideas in *How to Think Like a Scientist*. But there is only one main idea. Look again at the sentences you underlined. Write down one idea from each paragraph. Then write Kramer's main idea in the box.

Paragraph 1

Idea: Scientists are people who want to know about things around them.

Paragraph 2

Idea:

Paragraph 3

Idea:

Paragraph 4

Idea:

Paragraph 5

Idea:

Main Idea:

Scientists are people who:

23

Can you think like a scientist? Choose one thing to observe. It could be something outside the window, a class pet, or anything else that interests you. Make notes about your observation here.

24

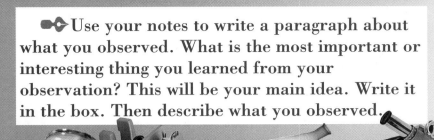

➨Use your notes to write a paragraph about what you observed. What is the most important or interesting thing you learned from your observation? This will be your main idea. Write it in the box. Then describe what you observed.

Main Idea:

25

When you read, look for the most important idea. This is called the main idea.

My Side of the Story

When you read, think about who is telling the story. When a character tells the story, we learn about that character's thoughts, hopes, and feelings. We see the world of the story from that character's **point of view**.

If the point of view changes, so does the story. In "The Three Little Pigs," the pigs are the good guys and the wolf is the villain, right? Not when the story is told from the wolf's point of view. As you read this piece from *The True Story of the Three Little Pigs*, circle places where the story is different from the version you know. In the Response Notes, write what you think really happened.

Response Notes

from *The True Story of the Three Little Pigs by A. Wolf*
as told to Jon Scieszka

But like I was saying, the whole Big Bad Wolf thing is all wrong. The real story is about a sneeze and a cup of sugar.

This is the real story.

Way back in Once Upon a Time time, I was making a birthday cake for my dear old granny. I had a terrible sneezing cold. I ran out of sugar.

So I walked down the street to ask my neighbor for a cup of sugar. Now this neighbor was a pig.

And he wasn't too bright, either.

He had built his whole house out of straw. Can you believe it? I mean who in his right mind would build a house of straw?

from *The True Story of the Three Little Pigs by A. Wolf*
as told to Jon Scieszka

So of course the minute I knocked on the door, it fell right in. I didn't want to just walk into someone else's house. So I called, "Little Pig, Little Pig, are you in?" No answer.

I was just about to go home without the cup of sugar for my dear old granny's birthday cake. That's when my nose started to itch. I felt a sneeze coming on. Well I huffed. And I snuffed.

And I sneezed a great sneeze.

And you know what? That whole straw house fell down. And right in the middle of the pile of straw was the First Little Pig—dead as a doornail.

He had been home the whole time.

Response Notes

27

●◆ How do you feel about the wolf now?

The story of the three pigs changes when it is told from A. Wolf's point of view. In the chart below, read what A. Wolf says happened. Then circle whether it is *True* or *False*. If you circle *False*, tell what you think really happened.

What A. Wolf Says Happened	What Really Happened
The wolf went to the pig's house to borrow a cup of sugar. True False	
Because the pig was not too bright, he built his house out of straw. True False	
The wolf called, "Little Pig, Little Pig, are you in?" True False	
The wolf huffed, and he snuffed, and he sneezed a great sneeze. True False	
The straw house fell down. True False	

28

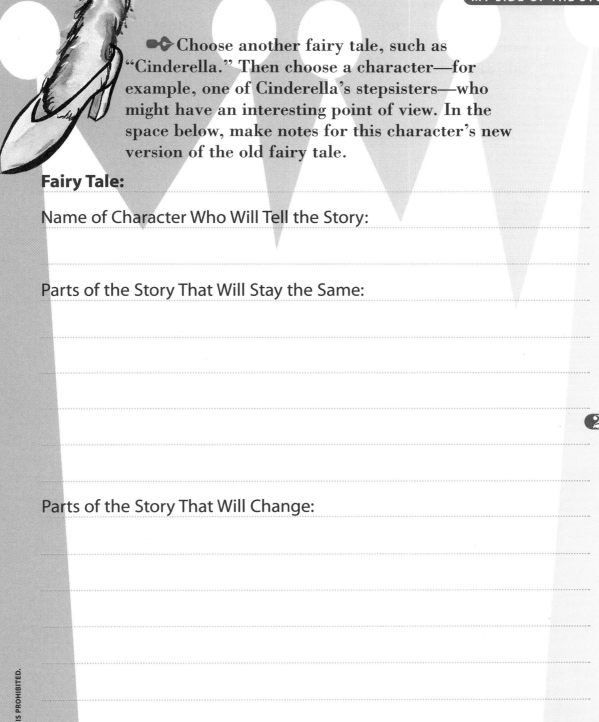

Choose another fairy tale, such as "Cinderella." Then choose a character—for example, one of Cinderella's stepsisters—who might have an interesting point of view. In the space below, make notes for this character's new version of the old fairy tale.

Fairy Tale:

Name of Character Who Will Tell the Story:

Parts of the Story That Will Stay the Same:

Parts of the Story That Will Change:

29

☞Use your notes from page 29 to rewrite a fairy tale. Keep some of the details from the real tale and add made-up details of your own.

Title ....

By ....
                    (character's name)

As Told To ....
                          (your name)

....

....

....

....

....

....

....

....

....

....

When the point of view
changes, the story changes too.

....

....

Reading Fiction

Some recipes are very, very simple. Think about lemonade, for example. All you need for lemonade is lemons, sugar, and water. If you have these three ingredients, you can make a good drink.

Writers of fiction also start with a simple recipe. Some of the most important ingredients for fiction are the characters, setting, and plot. If you have these three ingredients, you can make a good story.

In this unit, you'll learn about characters, setting, and plot. You'll find out how these ingredients work together to form a story.

Character Clues

Characters are an important part of any story. Watch what the characters **say** and **do**. Their actions and conversations can give you clues about what they're really like.

Read this story about a boy named Andrew. As you read, make predictions about Andrew in the Response Notes. Underline parts of the story that help you make your predictions.

Response Notes

from *Freckle Juice* by Judy Blume

After breakfast Andrew raced back to his bedroom. He opened his desk drawer and looked for a brown magic marker. All he could find was a blue one. It was getting late. Blue would have to do. He put the magic marker in his lunch box and headed for school. He stopped two blocks before he got there. He studied his reflection in a car window. Then he took out the magic marker and decorated his whole face and neck with blue dots. Maybe they didn't look like Nicky Lane's freckles, but they sure looked like something!

Andrew waited until the second bell rang. Then he hurried to his class and sat down. He took out a book and tried to read it. He heard a lot of whispering but he didn't look up.

Miss Kelly snapped her fingers. "Let's settle down, children. Stop chattering." Everybody giggled. "What's so funny? Just what is so *funny*? Lisa, can you tell me the joke?"

Response Notes

from *Freckle Juice* by Judy Blume

Lisa stood up. "It's Andrew, Miss Kelly. Just look at Andrew Marcus!"

"Stand up, Andrew. Let me have a look at you," Miss Kelly said.

Andrew stood up.

"Good heavens, Andrew! What have you *done* to yourself?"

"I grew freckles, Miss Kelly. That's what!" Andrew knew his blue dots looked silly but he didn't care. He turned toward Sharon and stuck out his tongue. Sharon made a frog face at him.

Miss Kelly took a deep breath. "I see," she said. "You may sit down now, Andrew. Let's get on with our morning work."

At recess Nicky Lane turned around and said, "Whoever heard of blue freckles?"

Andrew didn't answer him. He sat in class all day with his blue freckles. A couple of times Miss Kelly looked at him kind of funny but she didn't say anything. Then at two o'clock she called him to her desk.

"Andrew," Miss Kelly said. "How would you like to use my secret formula for removing freckles?" Her voice was low, but not so low that the class couldn't hear.

"For free?" Andrew asked.

"Oh yes," Miss Kelly said. "For free."

Andrew scratched his head and thought it over.

33

from **Freckle Juice** by Judy Blume

Miss Kelly took a small package out of her desk. She handed it to Andrew. "Now, don't open this until you get to the Boys' Room. Remember, it's a *secret formula*. Okay?"

"Okay," Andrew said.

He wanted to run to the Boys' Room, but he knew the rules. No running in the halls. So he walked as fast as he could. He couldn't wait to see what was in the package. Could there really be such a thing as freckle remover?

As soon as he was inside the Boys' Room he unwrapped the package. There was a note. Andrew read it. It said:

TURN ON WATER. WET MAGIC FRECKLE REMOVER AND RUB INTO FACE. RINSE. IF MAGIC FRECKLE REMOVER DOES NOT WORK FIRST TIME . . . TRY AGAIN. THREE TIMES SHOULD DO THE JOB.

MISS KELLY

Ha! Miss Kelly knew. She knew all the time. She knew his freckles weren't really freckles. But she didn't tell. Andrew followed Miss Kelly's directions. The magic freckle remover formula smelled like lemons. Andrew had to use it four times to get his freckles off. Then he wrapped it up and walked back to his classroom.

➥ Would you like to have a boy like Andrew in your class? Why or why not?

➥ Look back at the story. What did Andrew say and do?

What Andrew did with the blue marker:

What Andrew said to Miss Kelly:

What Andrew did with the secret formula:

➤ Write a journal entry about the day Andrew put blue dots on his face. Think about what Andrew said and did. Then *imagine* what he thought and felt.

Date _____

Where Am I?

Good readers gather bits and pieces of information as they read. Two important pieces of information have to do with the setting. **Setting** is the time (when the story takes place) and place (where the story happens).

As you read this story, circle information about *when* the story takes place. Highlight information about *where* the story takes place. Write down any questions you have about the setting in the Response Notes.

from *Two Girls in Sister Dresses*
by Jean Van Leeuwen

Jennifer loved everything about that house. She loved the big bedroom overlooking the ocean, where she woke up each morning to the soft whisper of waves on the sand. She loved the little kitchen that was always filled with people and good cooking smells. She loved the stone fireplace where Grandfather read stories after dinner, and the porch with its real swing hanging from the ceiling, and the path smelling of grass and buzzing with bees that led down to the beach.

But most of all, she loved the beach. The sand was white and warm and soft. You could dig in it, or build sand castles. At high tide waves came creeping up the sand, washing the sand castles away. At low tide you could walk out almost forever and the water still came only to your knees.

Response Notes

37

from *Two Girls in Sister Dresses*
by Jean Van Leeuwen

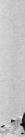

Or you could walk along the water's edge, where birds left tiny footprints in the damp gray sand, and pick up shells.

On a perfect summer afternoon, with puffs of white clouds gliding across a bright-blue sky, Jennifer sat on a beach blanket playing with her shells. Next to her sat Molly and their cousin, Sara Louise, who was just Molly's age. They were happily scooping and pouring sand, making cakes.

"Let's do another one!" Molly said each time they finished. And Sara Louise went off to the water for another pail of wet sand.

Nearby, under a striped umbrella, Jennifer's mother and Aunt Beth talked in low murmurs. And next to them the fathers were stretched out, reading, or maybe asleep. Up at the house, Jennifer's new baby cousin was asleep too, along with Grandmother and Grandfather, who always rested after lunch. And Aunt Virginia, the young aunt, was off somewhere with her friends. Everything was quiet.

Jennifer was thinking about waves. Where did they come from? Why were they sometimes little and ripply, like they were now, and other times big and crashing? Grandfather would know. She would ask him at dinnertime. And what would it feel like to ride a big wave, all by herself on her yellow raft?

🔑 Where does the story take place?

🔑 When does the story take place?

🔑 Write words that describe the setting of the story on the word web below. Write as many descriptive words as you can.

Example:

afternoon

39

Setting:

Two Girls in Sister

Dresses

Now think of a really wonderful day you once had. Picture where you were and when you were there. Then answer the questions below.

Where were you?

....

....

....

What made the day so special?

When were you there?

40

....

....

....

What were you doing?

Who was with you?

....

....

....

....

Use your star frame to help you draw a picture of the day you're thinking about. Make sure that your picture shows the "where" (place) and "when" (time) of your special day.

41

When you read a book or story, look for clues about setting.

What's Happening Here?

Did you know that you can't have a story without a plot? That's because the **plot** is the action. It is what happens in the story from the beginning to the end.

Read this story about a child who is afraid of the dark. As you read, watch for the events in the plot. Write any questions about what is happening in the Response Notes.

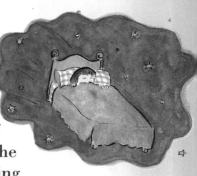

Response Notes

42

Señora Regañona
by Susana Sanromán

For ever so long I thought the night was a dreadful creature. I called her Señora Regañona.

I put a little light under my covers. Now I would sleep! She would never dare to come after me as long as the light shone bright. My glowing bed would even drive her out of my room. But my light kept me awake. I sat up and wondered, what is Señora Regañona doing up there in the dark?

Then one night I was so tired I forgot my light. I fell asleep. And while I slept I flew out into the starry adventure-filled sky. There I found Señora Regañona. I made her play with me.

We flew and floated over the houses. Down below were my safe bed and my safe house sleeping soundly while we played, my new friend, Señora Regañona, and I.

●◆ What event in the story surprised you?

●◆ Use this organizer to show the plot of *Señora Regañona*. Write the first thing that happens in the story in the first box. Write the next thing that happens in the next box, and so on. If you need to, add boxes on another sheet of paper.

1.

2.

43

3.

4.

5.

◆◆ Write a short book review of *Señora Regañona*. Use the notes from your organizer to help you describe what happened in the story. Then tell why you liked or did not like the story.

Book Review: <u>Señora Regañona</u>

<u>Señora Regañona</u>, by Susana Sanromán, is about

_____

_____

_____

_____

_____

This is how I felt about this story:

_____

_____

_____

_____

_____

_____

_____

Plot is what happens in the beginning, middle, and end of a story.

BLUE SKY
Clouds floating by
PASSING THROUGH THE TREES
gentle breeze
Poetry
O SUMMER!

Understanding Language

In this unit, you'll learn how to understand and enjoy the language of poetry. Poems come in all different shapes and sizes. Some poems are short. Others are long. Some poems explore one idea, while others tell a story. A poet may use simple words or fancy ones, small words or large.

Poets put a lot of thought into the words they use. When you come across a poem, try reading it aloud. Then ask yourself questions about the poem and the poet's language:
• What is the meaning of the poem?
• Do you like the way the words sound?
• Can you hear the poem's rhythm and rhyme?

Listening to a Poem

Poetry has a **rhythm,** or beat, just like music does. When you read a poem, listen for the beat. Is it a slow, dreamy beat or a fast, hip-hop beat?

Read this poem by Shel Silverstein. Underline the words that rhyme. Read the poem aloud to hear the rhythm. Can you hear where the rhythm in the poem changes? Make a big X in your Response Notes to show where you hear a change in rhythm.

Response Notes

Homework Machine by Shel Silverstein

The Homework Machine, oh the Homework Machine,

Most perfect contraption that's ever been seen.

Just put in your homework, then drop in a dime,

Snap on the switch, and in ten seconds' time,

Your homework comes out, quick and clean as can be.

Here it is—"nine plus four?" and the answer is "three."

Three?

Oh me . . .

I guess it's not as perfect

As I thought it would be.

☛ What did you like best about Shel Silverstein's poem?

➤ Look at where you marked an X in your Response Notes. As the rhythm changes, how does the feeling of the poem also change?

How does the child in the poem feel before X?

How does the child in the poem feel after X?

➤ Get ready to write a poem about a machine you'd like to invent. Follow these steps.

STEP 1 CHOOSE Decide what kind of machine you want to tell about in your poem.

My machine

STEP 2 EXPLAIN Write one or two sentences that tell what the machine does.

STEP 3 LIST List words that tell what the machine looks like and sounds like.

47

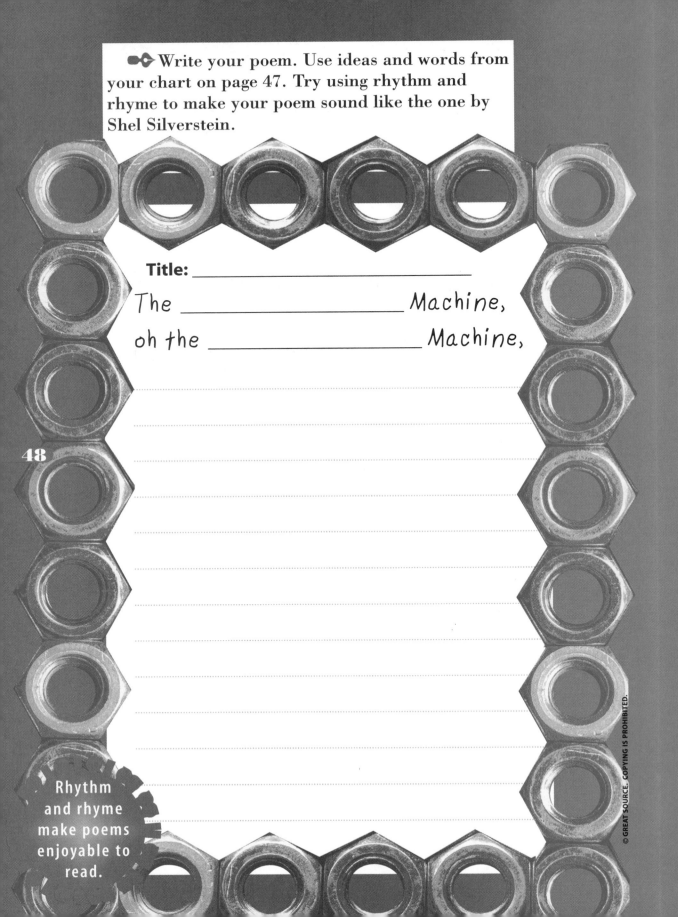

Write your poem. Use ideas and words from your chart on page 47. Try using rhythm and rhyme to make your poem sound like the one by Shel Silverstein.

Title: _____

The _____ Machine,

oh the _____ Machine,

48

Rhythm and rhyme make poems enjoyable to read.

Word Magic

Did you know that some poets spend hours choosing just the right word? This is because they know how important words can be. Sometimes poets choose words that help the reader picture what the poem is about.

Read this poem by Aileen Fisher. Circle words that help you picture the cricket in your mind. In the Response Notes, draw a sketch to go with one of the word pictures you circled.

Cricket Jackets by Aileen Fisher

The day a cricket's jacket
gets pinchy, he can crack it
and hang it on a bracket
as he goes hopping by.

He doesn't need a mother
to go and buy another,
he doesn't need a mother,
and I will tell you why:

Beneath the pinchy jacket
the cricket sheds with vigor
he has a new one growing
that's just a little bigger,
to last him till July.

And then, again, he'll crack it,
his pinchy cricket jacket,
and hang it on a bracket
as he goes hopping by.

Response Notes

49

☛ Think of an insect you would like to write about. Then tell why you chose this insect.

Insect:

I chose this insect because

☛ Aileen Fisher uses lots of great words—like *pinchy* and *vigor*—to describe how a cricket sheds its skin.

Make a word bank about your insect here. Try to come up with ten words. Remember to include words that help create a "picture" of your insect.

Word Bank

1.	6.
2.	7.
3.	8.
4.	9.
5.	10.

➥Now write a paragraph about your insect.
Use words from your word bank.
- First name what you are writing about.
- Then say what makes it interesting or special.

Sometimes writers choose words in order to help readers form pictures in their minds.

What's the Word?

What do you do when you're reading and you come across a word you don't know? Sometimes you can find the answer right on the page you're reading. Good readers know that they can look at nearby words to find clues about words they don't know. These clues are called **context clues.**

Read the poem below. Look at how one reader used context clues to figure out the meaning of the word *amiable*.

Response Notes

Example:

Huh? I never heard

of this word.

Hey, this dragon doesn't

sound very scary:

I wonder if amiable

means friendly?

I'm an Amiable Dragon
by Jack Prelutsky

I'm an amiable dragon,
And I have no wish to scare,
Do not tremble at my presence,
Do ignore my lethal stare,
Do not fret about the fire
I unleash into the air,
You are free to pass unchallenged
But only if you dare!

Now read another poem by Jack Prelutsky. Try to use context clues to figure out what the word *multilingual* means. Circle other words or phrases in the poem that might help you. In the Response Notes, write possible meanings for *multilingual*.

Response Notes

The Multilingual Mynah Bird
by Jack Prelutsky

Birds are known to cheep and chirp
and sing and warble, peep and purp,
and some can only squeak and squawk,
but the mynah bird is able to talk.

The mynah bird, the mynah bird,
a major, not a minor bird;
you'll never find a finer bird
than the multilingual mynah bird.

He can talk to you in Japanese,
Italian, French and Portuguese;
and even Russian and Chinese
the mynah bird will learn with ease.

The multilingual mynah bird
can say most any word he's heard,
and sometimes he invents a few
(a very difficult thing to do).

So if you want to buy a bird,
why don't you try the mynah bird?
You'll never find a finer bird
than the multilingual mynah bird.

53

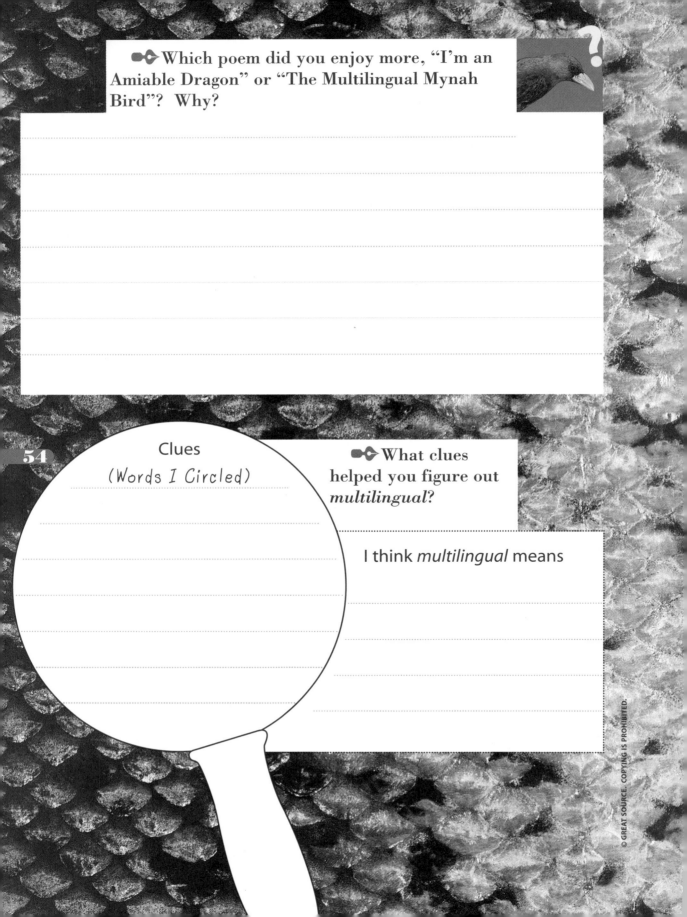

✏️ Which poem did you enjoy more, "I'm an Amiable Dragon" or "The Multilingual Mynah Bird"? Why?

Clues

(Words I Circled)

✏️ What clues helped you figure out *multilingual*?

I think *multilingual* means

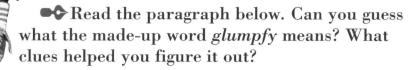

👉 Read the paragraph below. Can you guess what the made-up word *glumpfy* means? What clues helped you figure it out?

It takes my little brother an hour to eat his breakfast. He spends at least ten minutes tying his shoes! Then he walks to school like a snail. My brother is late everywhere he goes because he is so <u>glumpfy</u>.

👉 What clues helped you figure out *glumpfy?*

Clues
(Words I Circled)

I think *glumpfy* means

55

✏️ **Think up a made-up word of your own. Decide what you want the word to mean. Then use the word in a paragraph. Make sure your paragraph includes plenty of clues to help readers figure out the meaning of your made-up word.**

Made-up word: ....

Paragraph: ....

....

....

....

....

....

....

....

....

....

....

✏️ **Now let a friend read your paragraph. Was your friend able to figure out the meaning of your made-up word?**

Look for clues
when you come to
words you don't
know.

☐ Yes ☐ No

(HINT: If your friend had trouble figuring out the meaning of your word, try adding some more context clues to your paragraph.)

Reading Authors: Beverly Cleary

Beverly Cleary had a hard time learning to read as a child. She also couldn't find books she liked. "I wanted to read funny stories about the sort of children I knew," Cleary says. "I decided that someday when I grew up I would write them."

In Cleary's stories, the characters look, act, think, and feel like real children. When you read about characters like Ellen Tebbits and Henry Huggins, you might think to yourself, "That's just what I might do!"

In this unit, you'll look closely at Cleary's characters. You'll also look at Cleary's style, or the way she writes.

Finding Out About Characters

Every story has **characters**—people, animals, or made-up creatures. Good writers make a character seem real. They show how the character looks and acts. They describe the character's family or friends. They tell how the character thinks and feels.

Read this beginning of a story by Beverly Cleary about a third-grade girl. As you read, ask yourself: What does this character look like? What are her family and friends like? What does she like to do? Draw a star by parts of the story that answer these questions.

Response Notes

from *Ellen Tebbits* by Beverly Cleary

Ellen Tebbits was in a hurry. As she ran down Tillamook Street with her ballet slippers tucked under her arm, she did not even stop to scuff through the autumn leaves on the sidewalk.

The reason Ellen was in a hurry was a secret she would never, never tell.

Ellen was a thin little girl, with dark hair and brown eyes. She wore bands on her teeth and her hair was scraggly on the left side of her face, because she spent so much time reading and twisting a lock of hair around her finger as she read.

Response Notes

from **Ellen Tebbits** by Beverly Cleary

She had no brothers or sisters and, since Nancy Jane had moved away from next door, there was no one her own age living on Tillamook Street. So she had no really best friend. She did not even have a dog or cat to play with, because her mother said animals tracked in mud and left hair on the furniture.

Of course Ellen had lots of friends at school, but that was not the same as having a best friend who lived in the same neighborhood and could come over to play after school and on Saturdays. Today, however, Ellen was almost glad she did not have a best friend, because best friends do not have secrets from one another. She was sure she would rather be lonely the rest of her life than share the secret of why she had to get to her dancing class before any of the other girls.

The Spofford School of the Dance was upstairs over the Payless Drugstore. When Ellen came to the entrance at the side of the building, she paused to look anxiously up and down the street. Then, relieved that she saw no one she knew, she scampered up the long flight of steps as fast as she could run. There was not a minute to waste.

59

from _Ellen Tebbits_ by Beverly Cleary

She pushed open the door and looked quickly around the big, bare room. Maybe her plan was really going to work after all. She was the first pupil to arrive.

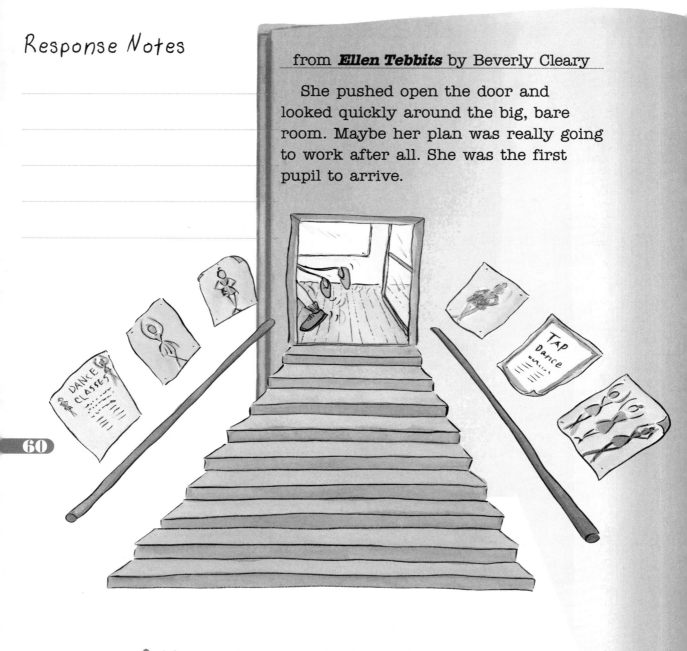

60

➥ **After reading the beginning of this story, what do you wonder about Ellen Tebbits?**

Fill in this chart about Ellen Tebbits by answering the questions. If you need help, look back at the places you starred in the story.

Questions	Your Answers
What does Ellen look like?	Thin Dark hair
What is Ellen's family like?	
What kinds of friends does Ellen have?	
What does Ellen like to do?	

61

✐ Write a character sketch of Ellen. A character sketch is a paragraph that describes a character. Use your chart to describe what Ellen looks like, what her family is like, what kinds of friends she has, and what she likes to do.

When you read, think about how characters look and act and what their lives are like.

How an Author Writes

Ballet slippers tucked under her arm . . .

Scuff through the autumn leaves on the sidewalk . . .

What do you notice about these phrases from Beverly Cleary's story *Ellen Tebbits?* When you read them, do pictures form in your mind? In her stories, Cleary includes words and details that make her writing interesting.

Read this beginning of the first story Beverly Cleary ever published. As you read, underline interesting descriptions and details.

63

from ***Henry Huggins***
by Beverly Cleary

Henry Huggins was in the third grade. His hair looked like a scrubbing brush and most of his grown-up front teeth were in. He lived with his mother and father in a square white house on Klickitat Street. Except for having his tonsils out when he was six and breaking his arm falling out of a cherry tree when he was seven, nothing much happened to Henry.

I wish something exciting would happen, Henry often thought.

But nothing very interesting ever happened to Henry, at least not until one Wednesday afternoon in March.

Response Notes

Response Notes

from *Henry Huggins* by Beverly Cleary

Every Wednesday after school Henry rode downtown on the bus to go swimming at the Y.M.C.A. After he swam for an hour, he got on the bus again and rode home just in time for dinner. It was fun but not really exciting.

When Henry left the Y.M.C.A. on this particular Wednesday, he stopped to watch a man tear down a circus poster. Then, with three nickels and one dime in his pocket, he went to the corner drugstore to buy a chocolate ice cream cone. He thought he would eat the ice cream cone, get on the bus, drop his dime in the slot, and ride home.

That is not what happened.

He bought the ice cream cone and paid for it with one of his nickels. On his way out of the drugstore he stopped to look at funny books. It was a free look, because he had only two nickels left.

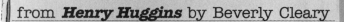

from *Henry Huggins* by Beverly Cleary

He stood there licking his chocolate ice cream cone and reading one of the funny books when he heard a thump, thump, thump. Henry turned, and there behind him was a dog. The dog was scratching himself. He wasn't any special kind of dog. He was too small to be a big dog but, on the other hand, he was much too big to be a little dog. He wasn't a white dog, because parts of him were brown and other parts were black and in between there were yellowish patches. His ears stood up and his tail was long and thin.

Response Notes

65

Draw a picture to go with one of the sentences you underlined as you read the story about Henry Huggins.

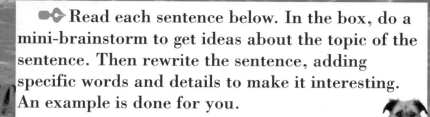

Read each sentence below. In the box, do a mini-brainstorm to get ideas about the topic of the sentence. Then rewrite the sentence, adding specific words and details to make it interesting. An example is done for you.

Sentence: The dog liked Henry.

Mini-Brainstorm Box

skinny   hungry   furry   jumped   wagged his tail   licked   excited   happy

New Sentence: The skinny dog was so happy to see Henry that he jumped up and licked his face.

Sentence: Henry liked the pool water.

67

Mini-Brainstorm Box

New Sentence:

Sentence: The bus driver was cranky.

Mini-Brainstorm Box

New Sentence:

Sentence: The ice cream was good.

Mini-Brainstorm Box

New Sentence:

Henry Huggins swims every Wednesday after school. What activities make up your after-school schedule? Choose a day of the week and complete the schedule below. Write a sentence describing what you usually do at about each time. Use specific words and details to help create a picture of each activity.

My After-School Schedule

Day:

Time	What I'm doing
4:00 P.M.	
5:00 P.M.	
6:00 P.M.	
7:00 P.M.	
8:00 P.M.	

5
6
69
8
9
10

Part of an author's style is the way he or she uses details to paint a picture in the

3 Writing About Real Life

The characters in Beverly Cleary's stories seem like real children. The things that happen in her stories seem like things that could happen in real life. Stories like Cleary's, which are made up but still seem real, are called **realistic fiction**.

In a book about her life called *My Own Two Feet*, Cleary tells how she got the ideas for her first story about Henry Huggins. She based the story partly on her own childhood in Portland, Oregon, where she had a best friend named Claudine. She also drew upon her experiences as a children's librarian in Yakima, Washington.

As you read the following passage, picture in your mind the neighborhood that Cleary describes. In the Response Notes, draw sketches of what you see in your mind.

Response Notes

from *My Own Two Feet*
by Beverly Cleary

How was I going to pull a story about boys from my imagination when I had spent so much of my childhood reading or embroidering? I recalled the Hancock Street neighborhood in Portland where I had lived when I was the age of the Yakima boys, a neighborhood where boys teased girls even though they played with them, where boys built scooters out of roller skates and apple boxes, wooden in those days, and where dogs, before the advent of leash laws, followed the children to school.

from *My Own Two Feet*
by Beverly Cleary

...Where Henry's name came from I do not know. It was just there, waiting to be written, but I do know Henry was inspired by the boys on Hancock Street, who seemed eager to jump onto the page. Hancock Street became Klickitat Street because I had always liked the sound of the name when I had lived nearby. I moved Claudine's house from Thirty-seventh Street to renamed Hancock Street to become Henry's house. When I came to the skinny dog who found Henry, I needed a name. We happened to have spareribs waiting in the refrigerator, so I named the dog Spareribs and continued the story, based on the family who took their dog home on a streetcar. I changed the family to one boy, and the streetcar into a bus.

What surprises you most about the way Beverly Cleary got her ideas?

Think about the kind of neighborhood that Cleary describes. Imagine it in your mind. Then draw either a scene from the neighborhood or a map of it, adding details of your own.

➥ Think about your own neighborhood. In the space below, write down some notes about what your neighborhood looks like, the children who live there, and the things that happen there.

What my neighborhood looks like:

Children in my neighborhood:

73

Things that happen in my neighborhood:

Choose your favorite ideas from the notes you made on page 73. Then write a beginning of a story in which you describe your neighborhood. Remember, it's okay to change some of the details or to add new, made-up ones.

Writers use their own experiences to create realistic characters, settings, and situations in stories.

75

Reading Well

Being able to read well is like having a key to a magical door. By opening the door, you can unlock the wonders of the real world and of the imagination.

In this unit, you'll read about the wonders of animals—both real and imaginary. You'll learn a lesson from a talking hen and find out about a giant bird-eating spider. As you read, you'll practice ways of opening the door to reading as wide as you can. You'll consider an author's purpose in writing, look for main ideas and details, and ask questions about what you read.

Why an Author Writes

Every author has a purpose, or reason, for writing. One author might write a funny story to entertain readers. Another might write a science book to inform or teach readers. Sometimes an author has more than one purpose in writing, such as to entertain *and* to teach readers.

As you read the following two stories by Arnold Lobel, ask yourself, "Why did the author write this story?" In other words, look for the **author's purpose.** In the Response Notes, write "entertain," or "teach" when you think you know the answer.

Response Notes

from ***Fables*** by Arnold Lobel

THE HEN AND THE APPLE TREE

One October day, a Hen looked out her window. She saw an apple tree growing in her backyard.

"Now that is odd," said the Hen. "I am certain that there was no tree standing in that spot yesterday."

"There are some of us that grow fast," said the tree.

The Hen looked at the bottom of the tree.

"I have never seen a tree," she said, "that has ten furry toes."

"There are some of us that do," said the tree. "Hen, come outside and enjoy the cool shade of my leafy branches."

The Hen looked at the top of the tree.

"I have never seen a tree," she said, "that has two long, pointed ears."

Response Notes

from **Fables** by Arnold Lobel

"There are some of us that have," said the tree. "Hen, come outside and eat one of my delicious apples."

"Come to think of it," said the Hen, "I have never heard a tree speak from a mouth that is full of sharp teeth."

"There are some of us that can," said the tree. "Hen, come outside and rest your back against the bark of my trunk."

"I have heard," said the Hen, "that some of you trees lose all of your leaves at this time of the year."

"Oh, yes," said the tree, "there are some of us that will." The tree began to quiver and shake. All of its leaves quickly dropped off.

The Hen was not surprised to see a large Wolf in the place where an apple tree had been standing just a moment before. She locked her shutters and slammed her window closed.

The Wolf knew that he had been outsmarted. He stormed away in a hungry rage.

It is always difficult to pose as something that one is not.

77

from *Fables* by Arnold Lobel

KING LION AND THE BEETLE

King Lion looked in the mirror.

"What a beautiful and noble creature I am," he said. "I will go forth to show my devoted subjects that their leader is every inch a king!"

The King put on his robes of state, his large jeweled crown, and all of his gold and silver medals. As he walked down the roads of his kingdom, everyone who saw him bowed to the ground.

"Yes, yes," said King Lion, "I deserve this respect from my people, for truly I *am* every inch a king!"

There was a tiny Beetle standing near the road.

When the King saw him, he cried, "Beetle, I command you to bow low before me!"

"Your Royal Majesty," said the Beetle, "I know that I am small, but if you look at me closely, you will see that I am making a bow."

The King leaned over.

"Beetle," he said, "you are so hard to see down there. I am still not sure that you are bowing."

"Your Majesty," said the Beetle, "please look more closely. I assure you that I am indeed bowing."

The King leaned over a little farther.

Response Notes

from **Fables** by Arnold Lobel

Now the robes of state, the large
jeweled crown, and all of the gold and
silver medals had made King Lion
very top-heavy. Suddenly he lost his
balance and fell on his head. With a
great roar, he rolled into a ditch at the
side of the road.

The frightened Beetle scurried
away. From head to foot, every inch
of King Lion was covered with wet
mud.

*It is the high and mighty who have
the longest distance to fall.*

79

●◆ Did you enjoy these stories? Why or why
not?

Fill in this chart about the two stories you read. For each story, write the author's purpose. Then tell what you learned from each story.

	"The Hen and the Apple Tree"	"King Lion and the Beetle"
Author's Purpose		
What I Learned from This Story		

"The Hen and the Apple Tree" and "King Lion and the Beetle" are both fables. Think about how the two stories are alike. Then use what you have learned from these stories to complete this sentence.

A fable is an animal story that

Imagine that Arnold Lobel is coming to your school. You get to interview the famous author. Write a list of questions that you would like to ask him about these fables.

1.

2.

81

3.

4.

As you read, ask yourself, "Why did the author write this?"

What's It All About?

As an active reader, look for the main idea of what you read. The **main idea** is the most important idea. It is what the selection is all about. Details are pieces of information that tell you more about the main idea. By finding the main idea and details about it, you will understand more of what you read.

Read this passage about fireflies. When you find the main idea, circle it. Highlight or underline any details about it.

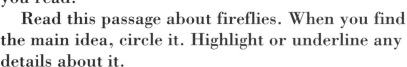

Response Notes

from ***Fireflies in the Night*** by Judy Hawes

I like fireflies. When I visit my grandfather in the summertime, we sit outdoors after supper and watch them.

Grandmother likes to watch fireflies too. She calls them lightning bugs. They look like little dancing stars. They are really beetles, Grandfather says.

All beetles have two sets of wings and so do fireflies. When they rest, they fold their hard front wings on top of their soft back wings.

Young fireflies do not have wings at all. For their first year or two they live in the ground, just like young beetles. When their wings grow, they live above ground in trees or bushes.

Grandfather gave me a glass jar to use on firefly hunts. We punched holes in the lid.

Fireflies are easy to catch. Soon my jar is lighted up like a lantern.

from **Fireflies in the Night** by Judy Hawes

After every firefly hunt, Grandfather has something new to tell me. One time he showed me how to make my firefly lantern brighter. (He promised it would not hurt my fireflies.) Just hold the jar upright in a bowl of warm water.

He knew it would work because fireflies always shine brighter in warm weather. If you dip the jar in cold water, the firefly lights will fade.

83

What did you learn about fireflies from reading this passage?

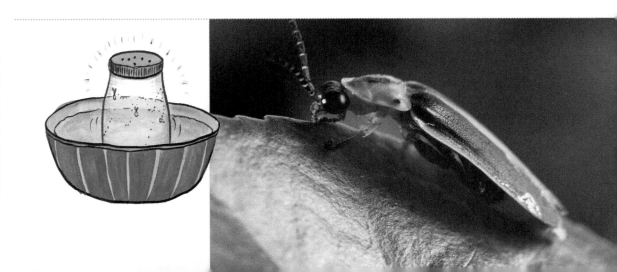

➡ In the organizer below, write the main idea of *Fireflies in the Night*. Then write 3 or 4 details that tell you more about the main idea.

detail

detail

main idea

detail

detail

84

Plan to write a paragraph of your own. Begin by finding a topic you know about. Write one sentence telling what you want to say about the topic. (This is your main idea.) Then write 3 or 4 details that support that idea.

topic

main idea

85

detail 1

detail 2

detail 3

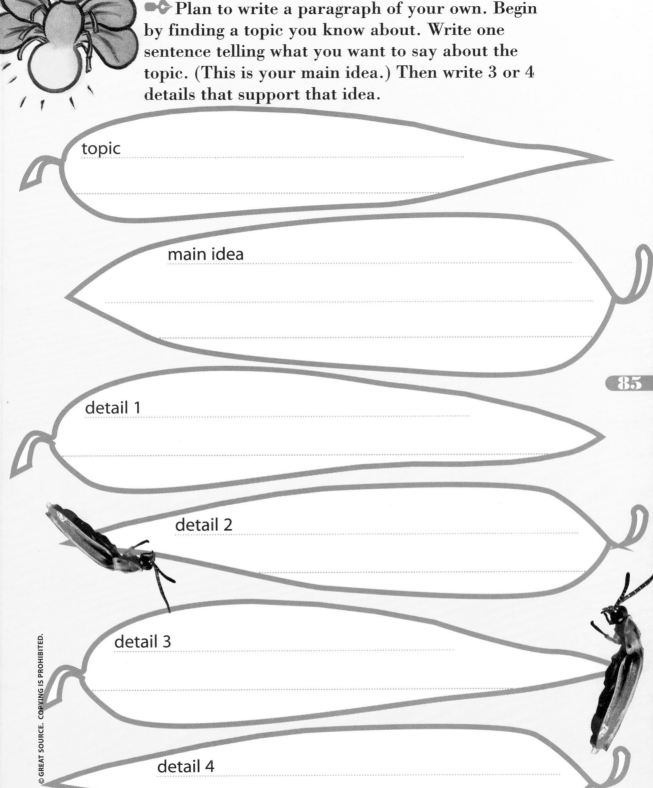

detail 4

Use your planner to write a paragraph about your topic. Begin with your main idea. Then add sentences with details about that idea.

86

When you read, look for the most important idea.

3 Using What You Know

When you read, you can use what you already know to learn more. First, look at the title and pictures to find out what the subject is. Then ask yourself two questions:

- What do I know about this subject?
- What do I want to find out?

Before you read the next passage, look at the book title and section title. Then start filling in the chart below. Write everything you know about large spiders in the first column. Then write down questions you have about the subject. The chart includes examples.

Topic: **Giant Spider**

K What I Know	W What I Want to Find Out	L What I Learned (Fill in this column after reading.)
I've seen spiders the size of a quarter.	How big is the largest spider in the world?	

Use the questions you listed in the chart to help focus your reading. Hunt for answers to the questions as you read. Draw a star by parts of the passage that answer your questions.

Response Notes

from ***Real Live Monsters!***
by Ellen Schecter

GIANT BIRD-EATING SPIDER
(Theraphosa leblondi)
Surinam

MEET THE MONSTER SPIDER: the largest in the world! Its body is nearly 4 inches long. Its leg span is up to 11 inches wide! It weighs almost as much as a quarter-pounder from McDonald's!

When it gets scared, this giant makes a purring noise. It rises up on its fourth pair of legs to look even larger! Its bite hurts, but isn't poisonous to humans.

This giant eats insects, small lizards, and small snakes (even poisonous ones). It also catches and eats small birds!

> In 1705, Maria Merian published a book of paintings she did in the Amazon jungle.
> One shows a huge spider dragging a hummingbird from its nest.
> Nobody believed her for **158 years . . . when another scientist finally *saw these spiders killing small birds*.**

from ***Real Live Monsters!***
by Ellen Schecter

This giant stabs its prey with poison fangs up to one inch long. Its venom turns the inside of its victim's body to liquid. Then it sips up the insides.

What do **you** think:
M-M-M-MONSTER?
Or just eating to live?

89

Return to the K-W-L Chart on page 87. In the last column of the chart, write what you learned.

What do you think is the weirdest fact about this giant spider?

✏️ Write a paragraph telling what you learned about the giant bird-eating spider. Use your chart to help you.

....

....

....

....

....

....

....

....

....

....

✏️ What questions do you still have about this topic? How or where could you find the answers?

....

....

....

....

....

Before you read, ask yourself: What do I already know about this subject? What do I want to know?

Reading Nonfiction

Nonfiction is writing about the real world. Some nonfiction tells true stories about people or events. Other nonfiction gives facts about a subject. By reading nonfiction, you can learn about people, places, and events from all over the world. You can find out about subjects as small as a mouse and as large as an elephant.

In this unit, you'll read about amazing animals, people, and places. And you'll learn ways to get more out of reading nonfiction. You'll learn to sum up what you read, to follow the order of events, and to get information from graphic aids, such as maps.

Sum It Up

When you read nonfiction, one goal is to understand and remember the most important ideas. One way to do this is to **summarize,** which means to tell the main ideas in your own words.

As you read this passage about elephants, underline the three or four ideas that you think are most important.

Response Notes

from **Safari** by Robert Bateman

Elephant

Elephants like to forage in forests where they can eat juicy young leaves and twigs from the treetops. You can hear them breaking off branches and munching. You can even hear the rumbling of their stomachs.

Because elephants are the largest land animals, they need to eat constantly. So an elephant herd is always on the move, looking for its next meal. A herd can travel as far as 40 miles (64 km) in one night.

No wonder elephants love to stop and cool down when they find water. In the heat of an African afternoon, one of the best places to look for elephants is at a watering hole or a river.

from **Safari** by Robert Bateman

ELEPHANT

Habitat: Forests, grasslands, river valleys
Height: Up to 14 ft. (4m)
Weight: 7,000–13,500 lb (3,000–6,250 kg)
Food: Vegetation, including fruit, leaves, bark, grass
Range: Southern, central and eastern Africa

The leader of an elephant herd is always the oldest female, known as the matriarch. She remembers where the deepest water holes are and knows the best places to find food.

The face of one of these wise, old female elephants makes me think of a map. The creases and wrinkles are like the mountains and rivers. The flat places are the wide plains.

Young male elephants do not live with the females and calves. Instead, they roam together in small groups. Sometimes they test their strength by fighting with each other.

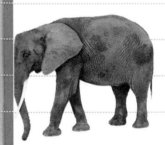

93

What fact about elephants do you find the most interesting? Why?

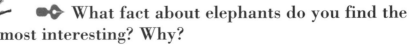

Look back at the information you underlined. Make an animal trading card by noting the facts under the headings below. Use your own words to write the information.

Facts about Elephants

Eating habits:

Size:

Where they live:

Leader of the herd:

Young male elephants:

�➤ Use your trading card notes to write a summary of the passage about elephants. Remember that a summary tells only the most important information.

95

A summary tells the most important ideas.

2 Tracking the Order of Events

True stories are often told as a **sequence of events,** which means in the order the events happened in time. Writers use words like *then, next,* and *later* to help readers follow the sequence of events. They also name specific times, such as "two years later" or "on November 1, 2000."

The following passage tells the true story of Helen Keller, who was blind and deaf. As you read, circle the words that give clues to the sequence of events, such as *then* and *later*.

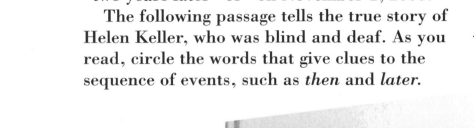

Response Notes

from ***A Picture Book of Helen Keller***
by David A. Adler

Helen's parents took her to eye doctors. But nothing could be done to help Helen see again.

Then Helen's parents took her to Washington, D.C. to meet Alexander Graham Bell, the inventor of the telephone. Dr. Bell had once taught in a school for the deaf. He helped the Kellers find a teacher for Helen.

The teacher they found was Anne Mansfield Sullivan. Helen first met her on March 3, 1887. Helen called that day her "soul's birthday."

Helen was not an easy student. Once, in a fit of anger, she knocked out two of Anne Sullivan's teeth.

from *A Picture Book of Helen Keller*
by David A. Adler

First Anne Sullivan taught Helen proper manners. Then she taught her words.

Anne used a finger alphabet. She gave Helen a doll and spelled "d-o-l-l" in the palm of Helen's hand. She gave Helen a hat and spelled "h-a-t" in her hand. But Helen did not understand.

One day Anne and Helen passed a water pump. Anne took Helen's hand and put it under the water. In Helen's other hand Anne spelled "w-a-t-e-r."

Now Helen understood. Everything has a name.

Helen wanted to learn more. That day she learned the words "mother" and "father." She also learned "teacher" which is what she called Anne Sullivan.

Many years later Helen Keller wrote that learning "water," her first word, gave her soul light, hope, and joy.

Helen learned hundreds, then thousands of words.

Soon Anne Sullivan taught Helen to read by feeling patterns of raised dots on paper. This kind of writing for the blind is called Braille.

Helen learned so much and so fast that she became famous throughout the world. She was called "the wonder girl."

97

B R A I L L E

📖➡ Look back over the passage you read. What is the sequence of events? Finish filling out the chart below to keep track of sequence.

On March 3, 1887

⬇

First *Anne Sullivan taught Helen*

⬇

One day *Anne and Helen*

⬇

Many years later

⬇

Soon *Anne Sullivan taught Helen*

➥ **Think about something you have done many times, such as getting ready for school. Describe the activity by telling what you do first, next, and so on. Be sure to include words like *then* and *next* to show the sequence.**

99

Understanding sequence helps you keep track of events.

Reading Maps, Charts, and Graphs

Sometimes the best way to get an idea across is with a map, chart, or graph. Nonfiction books that give facts about a subject often include these **graphic aids.** A graphic aid helps you see an idea. For example, a map helps you picture where a place is located.

Read this passage about places that hold world records. As you read, use the maps, charts, and graphs to create pictures of the facts in your mind.

Response Notes

from **Hottest, Coldest, Highest, Deepest**
by Steve Jenkins

The Nile, in Africa, is the longest river in the world. It is 4,145 miles long.

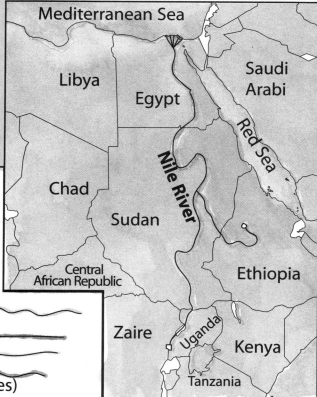

Mediterranean Sea

Libya

Egypt

Saudi Arabi

Red Sea

Chad

Nile River

Sudan

Central African Republic

Ethiopia

Zaire

Uganda

Kenya

Tanzania

United States
(2,750 miles wide)

Nile River (4,145 miles)
Amazon River (4,007 miles)
Chiang Jiang (3,964 miles)
Mississippi–Missouri (3,710 miles)

from ***Hottest, Coldest, Highest, Deepest***
by Steve Jenkins

Lake Baikal, in Russia, is the world's oldest and deepest lake. The lake was formed about 25 million years ago. In one spot it is 5,134 feet deep.

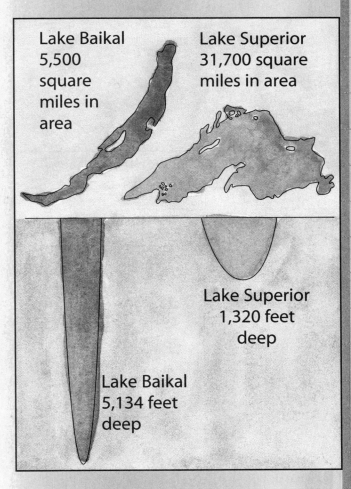

Lake Baikal
5,500 square miles in area

Lake Superior
31,700 square miles in area

Lake Superior
1,320 feet deep

Lake Baikal
5,134 feet deep

The largest freshwater lake in the world is Lake Superior, one of the Great Lakes in North America (31,700 square miles), but Lake Baikal (5,500 square miles) contains more water than any other lake on earth—more than all five Great Lakes combined.

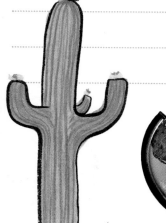

Response Notes

102

from ***Hottest, Coldest, Highest, Deepest***
by Steve Jenkins

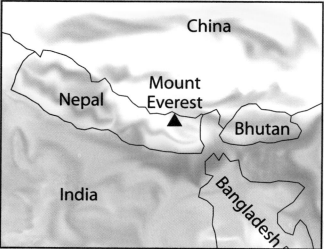

Mount Everest is the highest
mountain in the world. Its peak is
29,028 feet above sea level.

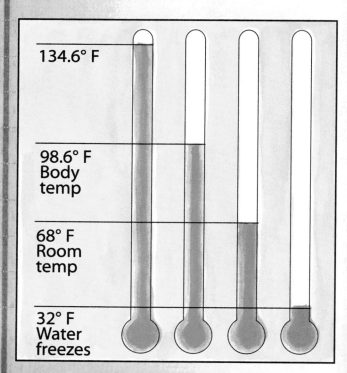

134.6° F

98.6° F
Body
temp

68° F
Room
temp

32° F
Water
freezes

The hottest temperature ever
recorded in the United States is
134.6° F, in Death Valley, California.

from *Hottest, Coldest, Highest, Deepest*
by Steve Jenkins

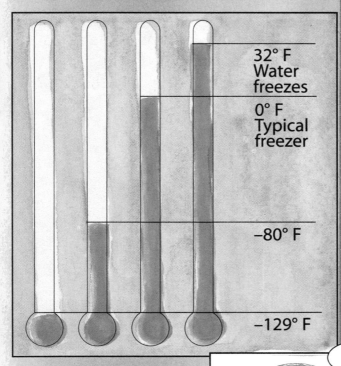

32° F
Water
freezes

0° F
Typical
freezer

−80° F

−129° F

Africa

South
America

Vostok,
Antarctica

The coldest place
on the planet is
Vostok, Antarctica.
A temperature of
129° F below zero
was recorded there.

Which of these world
record-breaking places would
you like to see? Why?

Try to answer these questions about your reading. Use the graphic aids on pages 100–103 to help you fill in the answers.

Compare the line lengths of the rivers on the chart on page 100. How many of the rivers are longer than the United States?

What countries does the Nile River run through?

In what country is Mount Everest?

How does the hottest temperature ever recorded compare with room temperature?

How does the coldest temperature ever recorded compare with the freezing temperature of water?

105

Find out the heights of each person in your family or several of your friends. Create a graphic aid, such as a bar graph, that will help a reader picture this information.

When you read nonfiction, use the graphic aids to help you picture ideas.

Understanding Language

Writers choose words carefully. Sometimes they choose words that make you, the reader, feel as if you are right there—smelling what the writer smells, hearing what the writer hears. These kinds of words are called **sensory details**. Other times writers compare two things in order to show how one thing is like another. These kinds of comparisons are called **similes**. Writers sometimes use words that make something that is not human seem human. This is called **personification**. As you read this unit, notice the words that the writers choose.

107

Hey, Reader—Are Your Senses Awake?

A writer uses **sensory details** to help you see, hear, feel, taste, or smell things the way the writer does. Sensory details work like this:

The cool rain gushed down on our heads.
Do you feel it?
The dog's steamy breath covered my face like a cloud. Can you see it? Smell it?

In *Great Crystal Bear,* author Carolyn Lesser uses many sensory details to make you see, hear, and feel the arctic wilderness. Read the passage. Then, circle any words that help you see, hear, feel, or smell the world of the great crystal bear.

Response Notes

108

Example:

I see fringy paws.

I feel cold snow.

Great Crystal Bear by Carolyn Lesser

Great crystal bear,

How do you survive on the thick ice

Covering the deep Arctic sea?

As you pad through the storm wind,

Veils of snow race past your fringy paws.

Time to scoop a hollow in a drift

And huddle in,

Back to the wind,

Nose pushed under the snow,

Paws snuggling your body.

Winds howl. Snow swirls,

Covering you like dust until you vanish.

Sleep warm, crystal bear.

Response Notes

Great Crystal Bear by Carolyn Lesser

The earth leans far from the sun

As you rouse from your drift-bed

This winter solstice morning.

How lucky that every other day of the year

Each hollow hair of your fur

Gathers sunlight

To heat your black skin and thick layer of fat.

Your blubbery blanket keeps you warm

For long, dog-paddling swims

And months of day-and-night

Winter wandering.

As you wander, great bear,

Your keen nose smells

Bear friends and relatives nearby.

Some nap behind hills of ice.

Others travel.

They are like you,

Comforted by the scent of companions

But on singular journeys,

Alone, but not lonely.

◆➤A great crystal bear is white, the color of snow. Could you see his face? What do you think he might look like? In the space below, draw a picture of the crystal bear. Use the words you circled to help you picture the bear.

Think of an animal *you* could describe. Think of how it looks, sounds, smells, or feels when you touch it. Use the chart below to brainstorm a list of sensory details.

Kind of Animal:

Looks like:

Sounds like:

Smells like:

Feels like:

111

➡️ Write a short paragraph that describes your animal. Use sensory details from your chart to make your paragraph interesting.

Sensory details help the reader imagine what the writer describes.

Understanding Similes

Her eyes were as big as dinner plates!

Can you picture eyes that big? If you can, you know the power of a simile. A simile is a writer's way of comparing two things—like eyes and dinner plates—that we might not usually think of together. Similes help make a writer's meaning clear. Similes use the words *like* or *as* to compare:

Her face was <u>as</u> round and smooth <u>as</u> a balloon.

His hair stuck straight up, <u>like</u> fresh mown grass.

In *Angels in the Dust,* the author uses many similes to help readers understand what it was like to live in Oklahoma during a time when the dust would not stop blowing. As you read, highlight all the similes you can find. In the Response Notes, jot down the two things being compared.

from ***Angels in the Dust***
by Margot Theis Raven

Time was, children, when I was a young girl, I lived on a wheat farm, as flat as a breadboard. The farm was on the Panhandle plains of Oklahoma. That's where the land reaches out straight as a handshake, like the end of a pot.

Our little house on the farm was small and brown. It had only two rooms and a lean-to kitchen for Mama, Papa, Bessie, and me. I was the oldest and I was named after Mama, because Papa said I had Mama's eyes—as big and blue as a bowl of prairie sky.

Response Notes

from *Angels in the Dust*
by Margot Theis Raven

When I was twelve and Bessie was six, our sky, so big and blue, turned dark and fierce in the middle of the day. Great dust storms came blowing. They came with the drought that took hold of the land. No rain fell for a long, long time.

Mean new winds came blowing, too, scorching hot and stiff as a dragon's breath. They withered our corn. They withered our wheat. They baked our land bone-dry until it looked as cracked and old as Mama's white milk pitcher. Soon nothing grew in Papa's fields except great piles of dusty earth.

When those dust winds blew at night, dirt came right through the cracks in our little brown house. Before bed Bessie and I always stuffed the cracks with old newspaper scraps and hung wet sheets over the windows to keep the dirt from blowing in. Still it came to call like an unwanted visitor. It covered our faces with sandy grit as we slept, and in the morning our pillows would be brown, except for the spots where our heads had been.

114

from *Angels in the Dust*
by Margot Theis Raven

Most mornings, too, we'd find the dust from the night lying sandy and dark across the kitchen table. After chores I liked to trace my name in the dirt as if it were a chalkboard. Sometimes I helped Bessie write out her name, pretending I was a teacher. Mama always smiled when she saw me giving lessons in the dust.

"Annie," she'd say, "you make me think nothing's so bad that it isn't good for something."

What was it like to live in Oklahoma during a time of huge dust storms? Look back at the similes you marked. Pick one that really sticks in your mind. Draw a picture to show what you see in your mind when you read this simile.

115

How could wind be like a dragon's breath? Explain. Reread page 114 if you're not sure.

You can create similes of your own. Fill in the blanks for the first two. Then, see if you can make up two similes of your own. Use the words *as* and *like* to help you.

1. The horse ran *like*

2. The old man's hands were *as* rough *as*

3.

4.

◗◆ Think of a person or place you know very well. Write a short description of that person or place. Use at least one simile in your description. (Use more than one if you can!)

117

Similes make meaning clear by showing how one thing is like another.

3 When Animals Talk

Personification is an author's way of making something that is not human seem human. When authors create animals that talk and act like people do, they are using **personification**.

Byrd Baylor uses personification to describe several animals in her book *Desert Voices*. As you read, underline any clues that help you predict what kind of animal might be speaking. After each stanza, stop and write a prediction in the Response Notes.

Response Notes

---

from ***Desert Voices*** by Byrd Baylor

I move so flat against
the earth
that I know all
its mysteries.

I understand
the way sun
clings to rocks
after the sun is gone.

I understand
the long cold shadows
that wrap themselves
around me
and slow my blood
and call me back
into the earth.

from **Desert Voices** by Byrd Baylor

On the south side of
a rocky slope
where sun can warm
my hiding place,
I wait for the cold
that draws me into
sleep.

I understand
waking
in spring,
still cold,
hardly moving,
seeking warmth,
seeking food,
going from darkness
to light.

from **Desert Voices** by Byrd Baylor

I understand
the shedding
of old skin
and the tenderness
of my new soft shining
self
flowing
smooth as water
over sand.

I understand
the sudden strike,
the death I hold
behind my fangs.

Wherever I go
I cast
a shadow of fear.

🔹➤ What kind of animal do you think is speaking?

_____

🔹➤ How do you know?

_____

_____

🔹➤ Pretend you are an animal. Try to picture yourself as this animal. List four things that are special about you.

1. _____

2. _____

3. _____

4. _____

_____

◖◆ Now, write a short paragraph that describes what you are like as an animal. Tell the world what it is like to be you. When you're finished, read what you wrote to a friend. Can your friend guess what animal you are?

Writers make stories come to life by giving animals and objects human qualities.

Reading Authors: Patricia McKissack

Award-winning author Patricia McKissack grew up in a family full of storytellers. When she became a writer, she remembered the stories she had heard as a child. She remembered strong characters that seemed like real children. She remembered the colorful way her grandfather used language. She knew she wanted her stories to have these same qualities.

As you read Patricia McKissack's writing, think about the people and stories that were important to her as a child. Pay close attention to her characters, and notice the way she uses language.

Characters Make the Story

Can you imagine a story with *no* characters at all? No one *speaking*? No one *doing anything*? How dull! Characters make a story interesting—especially if they are interesting themselves.

In "Monday," we meet two characters: Ma Dear and David Earl. As you read the story, ask yourself, "What are these two people like?" Underline words or phrases that tell you what they are like. In the Response Notes, write down comments or questions about Ma Dear and David Earl.

Response Notes

124

"Monday" from *Ma Dear*
by Patricia McKissack

David Earl knows it's Monday, because Ma Dear puts on her blue apron, the one with the long pocket across the front. It's wash day, and that's where she keeps the clothespins.

First, Ma Dear heats water in the big kettle and pours it into several tubs. Then she rolls up her sleeves and scrubs each piece on her rub board. David Earl would rather blow bubbles, but instead he gathers peach tree leaves for Ma Dear to use in the last rinse.

"That's the secret to my bright wash," Ma Dear explains as they hang out sheets.

At day's end, when the last sweet-smelling piece has been taken off the line and folded, Ma Dear rests in her rocking chair. Her hands are red and chafed. She's so tired, yet she holds out her arms. "Come," she says.

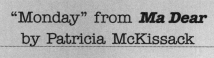

"Monday" from *Ma Dear*
by Patricia McKissack

Response Notes

David Earl crawls into his mother's lap. She reaches inside her blue apron pocket and takes out a wooden clothespin. "Once there was a brave soldier . . . ," she begins. The clothespin becomes that soldier standing at attention. " . . . who died fighting out West."

David Earl looks at the flag and sword hanging over the mantel. "His name was Sgt. David Earl Bramlett, Sr.—the same as mine, except I'm a junior," he adds, finishing the story he's heard many times before.

Too soon it's time for bed. Ma Dear kisses her son good night, and he drifts off to sleep, wrapped in a wind-dried sheet that smells of peach blossoms.

125

■◆ What kind of person is Ma Dear?
Brainstorm as many words as you can think of to
describe her.

Kind

Ma Dear

■◆ What kind of person is David Earl?
Brainstorm as many words as you can think of to
describe him.

Helpful

David Earl

How do you picture Ma Dear in the story? What are her eyes like? Is she smiling, or frowning, or sad, or serious? What about David Earl? Draw a sketch of one of the characters to show how you see that character's face.

127

A journal is a book of notes you write to yourself. Pretend you are the character you sketched—either Ma Dear or David Earl. It is the end of the day and you are thinking back on your Monday. What might you write in your journal?

This journal belongs to:

Interesting characters talk, act, and feel like real people.

What's My Purpose?

Authors write for many reasons: to tell a story, give information, convince a reader something is true, or share thoughts and feelings. Knowing the author's purpose helps you understand what the author is trying to say.

Read Patricia McKissack's "Author's Note" from *Ma Dear*. Some things she says may remind you of that story. As you read, highlight any clues that help you figure out McKissack's purpose for writing *Ma Dear*.

from *Ma Dear* by Patricia McKissack

AUTHOR'S NOTE

I recently inherited a plain muslin apron that had belonged to Leanna, my great-grandmother. And although the design is ordinary, the woman who wore it was not. Ma Dear (a short form of mother dear), as Leanna was affectionately called, was a single parent who raised three children in rural Alabama in the early 1900s. She made a living cooking, cleaning, washing, and ironing for other people. These were back-breaking chores, more difficult, of course, because there were no electric irons, washing machines, or other modern appliances. And the pay was very low. My grandmother often told me about her remarkable mother, who worked hard yet always found time for her children and grandchildren—sharing funny stories, teaching them songs, playing games—no matter how tired and sore she was. Those memories inspired me

Response Notes

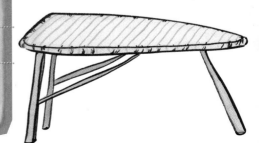

from **Ma Dear** by Patricia McKissack

to write this story, in which the real Ma Dear's stories, songs, and games are included.

Here, then, is my tribute to my great-grandmother—and also the countless other domestic workers of her generation. For them the apron was a convenient, all-purpose tool, used to carry wood and kindling, to gather eggs and vegetables, to wipe their brows in the noon-day sun, or just to hide a special treat for a willing helper.

Patricia C. McKissack
St. Louis, Missouri
1997

130

●◆Why is Ma Dear's plain muslin apron special to Patricia McKissack?

●◆Look carefully at the clues you underlined about Patricia McKissack's purpose. Why do you think she wrote the book *Ma Dear* about her great-grandmother?

In her author's note, Patricia McKissack writes that *Ma Dear* is a tribute to her great-grandmother, Leanna. A *tribute* is a way of honoring or thanking someone special.

Think of someone who is special to you. Then, in the space below, plan a tribute to that person.

My special person is:

Reasons this person is important to me:

131

Think of one special thing—like Ma Dear's apron—that reminds you of this person:

Write a tribute to your special person. Use your notes from page 131. When you finish, you may want to give the person you wrote about a copy of your tribute.

A tribute to

By

When you know a writer's purpose, it can help you make sense of what you read.

3 An Author's Language

In her autobiography, Patricia McKissack writes about the way she uses words and language in her books:

"I imagine I'm listening to my grandfather tell one of his tales. He had such a special way of saying things.

'I disremember ever seeing a fox . . .,' said Flossie.

'Be particular 'bout them eggs,' said Big Mama.

I want my characters to use the same colorful language of the rural South that Daddy James used."

As you read *Mirandy and Brother Wind*, pay special attention to the way characters talk. Circle the words and phrases you like. Put question marks by any words or phrases you have questions about.

133

from *Mirandy and Brother Wind*
by Patricia McKissack

Swish! Swish!

It was spring, and Brother Wind was back. He come high steppin' through Ridgetop, dressed in his finest and trailing that long, silvery wind cape behind him.

Swoosh! Swoosh! Swoosh!

"Sure wish Brother Wind could be my partner at the junior cakewalk tomorrow night," say Mirandy, her face pressed against the cool cabin window. "Then I'd be sure to win."

Response Notes

from *Mirandy and Brother Wind*
by Patricia McKissack

Ma Dear smiled, "There's an old saying that whoever catch the Wind can make him do their bidding."

"I'm goin' to," say Mirandy. And she danced around the room, dipping, swinging, turning, wheeling. "This is my first cakewalk. And I'm gon' dance with the Wind!"

When the sky turned morning pink, Mirandy set out to capture Brother Wind. Grandmama Beasley was out back feeding her chickens when Mirandy come up asking all excited, "Do you know how to catch Brother Wind? I want to make him be my partner at the cakewalk tonight."

Grandmama Beasley studied on the notion. "Can't nobody put shackles on Brother Wind, chile. He be special. He be free."

Mirandy asked all her neighbors the same question, but nobody seemed to have an answer.

"I'm gon' get him yet," she say, turning 'round and 'round in the yard.

FIRST PRIZE
FOR
DANCE CONTEST

Pick your favorite description of Brother Wind in the story. Write how McKissack describes him. Then draw an illustration to go with the words.

© GREAT SOURCE. COPYING IS PROHIBITED.

🔖 Choose one of these sentences from *Mirandy and Brother Wind*. Then rewrite the sentence using your own words.

Grandmama Beasley studied on the notion.

"Can't nobody put shackles on Brother Wind, chile."

"I'm gon' get him yet," she say, turning 'round and 'round in the yard.

🔖 Think about how you talk when you're with your best friends. What are some special words or phrases you use? Write them here:

➤ Now imagine you are having a conversation with one of your friends. Write down what each person would say. Remember to use words that sound like the way real people talk.

137

Good writers make their characters sound like real people.

Text

10 From *A Mouse Called Wolf* by Dick King-Smith. Copyright © 1997 by Fox Busters Ltd. Reprinted by permission of Crown Children's Books, a division of Random House, Inc.

14 "A Fire-Breathing Dragon" by Douglas Florian from *Bing, Bang, Boing,* copyright © 1994 by Douglas Florian, reprinted by permission of Harcourt, Inc.

16 From *Solomon the Rusty Nail* by William Steig. Copyright © 1985 by William Steig. Reprinted by permission of Farrar, Straus and Giroux, LLC.

21 From *How to Think Like a Scientist* by Stephen Kramer. Text copyright © 1987 by Stephen P. Kramer.

26 From *The True Story of the Three Little Pigs by A. Wolf* by Jon Scieszka, copyright © 1989 by Jon Scieszka. Used by permission of Viking Penguin, a division of Penguin Putnam, Inc.

32 From *Freckle Juice* by Judy Blume. Reprinted with the permission of Simon & Schuster Books for Young Readers, an imprint of Simon and Schuster Children's Publishing Division. Text copyright © 1971 Judy Blume.

37 From *Two Girls in Sister Dresses* by Jean Van Leeuwen, copyright © 1994 by Jean Van Leeuwen Gavril. Used by permission of Dial Books for Young Readers, a division of Penguin Putnam, Inc.

42 *Señora Regañona,* text copyright © 1997 by Susan Sanromán. English translation copyright © 1998 by Groundwood Books/Douglas & McIntyre. Reprinted by permission of the publisher.

46 "Homework Machine" by Shel Silverstein. Copyright © 1981 Evil Eye Music, Inc. Used by permission of HarperCollins Publishers.

49 "Cricket Jackets" by Aileen Fisher. First published in *Cricket, The Magazine for Children,* November, 1973. Copyright © by Aileen Fisher.

52 "I'm an Amiable Dragon" by Jack Prelutsky form ZOO DOINGS. Copyright © 1993 by Jack Prelutsky.

53 "The Multilingual Mynah Bird" by Jack Prelutsky from ZOO DOINGS. Copyright © 1983 by Jack Prelutsky.

58 From *Ellen Tebbits* © 1951 by Beverly Cleary.

63 From *Henry Huggins* © 1950 by Beverly Cleary.

70 From *My Own Two Feet* © 1995 by Beverly Cleary.

76 "The Hen and the Apple Tree" and "King Lion and the Beetle" from FABLES by Arnold Lobel.

82 From *Fireflies in the Night* by Judy Hawes. Text copyright © Judy Hawes, copyright renewed © 1991 by Judy Hawes. Used by permission of HarperCollins Publishers.

88 From *Real Live Monsters!* by Ellen Schecter © Bank Street College of Education.

92 "Elephant" by Robert Bateman. Text by Rick Archbold and The Madison Press Limited © 1998 from SAFARI, a Little Brown & Co./Madison Press Book.

96 From *A Picture Book of Helen Keller* by David A. Adler. Text copyright © 1990 by David A. Adler. All rights reserved. Reprinted from A PICTURE BOOK OF HELEN KELLER by permission of Holiday House, Inc.

100 Excerpts from *Hottest, Coldest, Highest, Deepest* by Steve Jenkins. Copyright © 1998 by Steve Jenkins. Reprinted by permission of Houghton Mifflin Company. All Rights Reserved.

108 From *Great Crystal Bear,* text copyright © 1996 by Carolyn Lesser, reprinted with permission from Harcourt, Inc.

113 From *Angels in the Dust* by Margot Theis Raven. Copyright © 1997 by Margot Raven. Published by and reprinted with permission of Troll Communications L.L.C.

118 "Desert Tortoise" by Byrd Baylor and Peter Parnall. Reprinted with the permission of Atheneum Books for Young Readers, an imprint of Simon & Schuster Children's Publishing Division from DESERT VOICES by Byrd Baylor and Peter Parnall. Text copyright © Byrd Baylor.

124, 129 "Monday" from *Ma Dear* and "Author's Note" by Patricia McKissack. Reprinted with the permission of Atheneum Books for Young Readers, an imprint of Simon & Schuster Children's Publishing Division, from MA DEAR'S APRONS by Patricia C. McKissack. Text copyright © 1997 Patricia McKissack.

133 From *Mirandy and Brother Wind* by Patricia McKissack. Copyright © 1988 by Patricia C. McKissack. Reprinted by permission of Alfred A. Knopf Children's Books, a Division of Random House, Inc.

Book Design: Christine Ronan and Sean O'Neill, Ronan Design

Cover Photographs: Stream, © Peter Griffith/Masterfile; Frog, © Tim Davis/Stone

Illustrations on pages 9, 15, 31, 45, 57, 75, 91, 107, 123 © Lisa Adams. Illustration on page 46 © Shel Silverstein. All other illustrations © Marian Nixon

Photograph of spider eating bird on page 89 © J. Mitchell/Animals Animals

Photo Research and **Text Permissions**: Feldman and Associates

Developed by Nieman Inc.

The editors have made every effort to trace the ownership of all copyrighted selections found in this book and to make full acknowledgement for their use. Omissions brought to our attention will be corrected in a subsequent edition.

autobiography, a true story written by a person about his or her own life.

author's purpose, the reason why an author writes.

biography, a true story written by one person about another person's life.

brainstorm, to jot down thoughts about a subject in order to get ideas for writing.

character, a person, animal, or imaginary creature in a story.

context clues, using the words and sentences around an unknown word to figure out the word's meaning.

details, in nonfiction, facts and examples that are used to support the main idea. In fiction, words and description that add interest to writing.

dialogue, talking between characters in a story.

fable, a short story that is written to teach a lesson.

fiction, writing that tells an imaginary story.

graphic aid, pictures that help readers understand facts, ideas, and information. Graphic aids include graphs, charts, maps, and diagrams.

highlight, a way to mark the information during reading that is most important or that you want to remember.

inferences, using details from reading and what you already know to understand what you read.

interview, to collect information by asking a person a series of questions.

journal, a written record of thoughts, feelings, and ideas.

K-W-L, a reading strategy that focuses on what the reader already <u>knows</u> (K), what the reader <u>wants</u> to find out (W), and what the reader <u>learned</u> (L).

main idea, the most important point in a piece of writing.

metaphor, a comparison that does not use the word *like* or *as.*

nonfiction, writing about real people, places, things, or ideas.

paragraph, a group of sentences that tell about one subject or idea.

personification, a figure of speech in which an idea, object, or animal is given human qualities.

plot, the action of the story.

poetry, a special kind of writing in which words are chosen and arranged to create a certain effect.

point of view, the angle from which a story is told.

predict, using what you already know and story clues to guess what will happen next.

prior knowledge, using what you already know to understand what you read.

realistic fiction, a story that seems as if it could be real although it is not true.

rhyme, repeated sounds at the ends of words.

rhythm, the beat in spoken language or in writing.

sensory details, words and examples that help the reader see, feel, smell, taste, and hear a subject.

sequence, the order in which events happen.

setting, the time and place of the story.

simile, a comparison that uses the word *like* or *as.*

141

summarize, writing or telling only the most important ideas from something you have read.

synonym, a word that means about the same thing as another word.

theme, the message or point of a piece of writing.

topic, the subject of a piece of writing.

visualize, to see or picture in your mind what you read.

142

143